The Letter Box and other Stories

To nourish the mind and soul

Charu Gupta

Om Books International

First published in 2025

Om Books International

Corporate & Editorial Office
A-12, Sector 64, Noida 201 301
Uttar Pradesh, India
Phone: +91 120 477 4100
Email: editorial@ombooks.com
Website: www.ombooksinternational.com

Sales Office
107, Ansari Road, Darya Ganj,
New Delhi 110 002, India
Phone: +91 11 4000 9000
Email: sales@ombooks.com
Website: www.ombooks.com

Cover Design: Charu Gupta

ISBN: 978-93-63953-48-2

Printed in India

10 9 8 7 6 5 4 3 2 1

This book is a tribute to my father
Dr Ashwini Kumar Gupta,
who was and shall always remain
my highest pillar of strength.

Acknowledgements

I am truly and deeply grateful to my children Aarush and Rithanya for having been enthusiastic listeners to my stories and for inspiring my creativity and imagination;

My husband Arvind Bansal, whose constant motivation helped me in penning down my passion to narrate engaging stories into a written treasure;

All the people in my life whose virtues or vices have inspired me to write these stories;

Mr Ajay Mago, Publisher, Om books International who believed in my writing and ensured its journey to the hands of the readers;

Last but not the least, Senior Editor Dr Kirti Pathak for her brilliant inputs and insights that helped in making my stories even more impactful.

Thank you, each one of you.

Contents

The Pilgrimage

It was the onset of winter and there was a chill in the air. Donning only a shawl around his chest, Ram Narayan, an obsessively religious old man, could be heard chanting mantras inside the local temple. The lamp in his hand could be seen dancing to the jingle of the bell in his other hand. Dawn was about to crack and Ram Narayan was deeply engrossed in his devotion. Being a learned and well-versed Sanskrit scholar, he was acknowledged and revered by the entire village. With the passage of time, this recognition surrounded him with an air of superiority and arrogance. The episode of his leaving a nuptial ceremony for not having being paid enough respect was well known in the vicinity.

"Babu ji, babu ji!" shouted an unknown voice at his door as soon as he returned home. An annoyed Ram Narayan came out to inquire the issue. It was Gopal, a poor villager who had come to invite Ram Narayan to his daughter's wedding and bless her. "Not at this time Gopal," firmly replied Ram Narayan. "But... babu ji, I have come to you with a lot of hope. My daughter will not be happy in life if you don't bless her. Her marriage may fail, or she may have to undergo too much suffering, or may be she does not experience marital bliss...." Gopal kept requesting with folded hands. Ram Narayan ignored his pleas and went inside. He replied from inside, "Arrey, I am going on a pilgrimage and will be back after ten days."

Ram Narayan was certainly excited and had stuffed his bag with everything he thought he would require in the course of his journey. From his favourite woolen sweater that he had received as a gift last year, to his new shoes—he ensured he missed nothing. His medicines, some snacks to eat, his sacred praying beads and his religious texts had all been packed. Ram Narayan had to catch his train at ten in the morning. Usually his early morning routine could not keep him in bed beyond 4 am, but today he was awake much earlier, rather he did not sleep at all out of excitement.

After duly performing his mandatory rituals, Ram Narayan cooked some brinjals and some chapatis, ate two of them and carefully packed the remaining food for his journey. He quickly checked if he had kept with him all his prized possessions, including his grandmother's silver coin. Some cash was safely hidden in a secret pocket stitched inside his neatly ironed silk kurta, and the remaining amount lay deep inside the *dal*, tea and flour containers. Ram Narayan was juggling with mixed emotions of nervousness and excitement all at once. He ensured twice that the wooden doors of his house were properly locked. Finally, before taking his last step out of the porch, he silently murmured a mantra and without wasting another moment, called a rickshaw puller to take him to the station. Though the station wasn't far away and could be reached even by the local bus, Ram Narayan didn't mind spending an extra five rupees for the ride. Today he was in a different mood altogether. His chin was raised in pride and his eyebrows lifted, as if he were an emperor out to conquer the enemy army. He waved with an attitude and a royal smile as he raised his folded hands in response to the greetings of people passing by. Soon, the serenity of the village seemed to lose itself to the brawling crowd and indiscreet chatters, announcing that the station had arrived.

Ram Narayan carefully stepped down the rickshaw, paid five rupees to the rickshaw puller, and headed towards the platform. Making his way through the crowd, he boarded the train and took his seat. It was to be a long journey so he purchased a local newspaper to avoid the unnecessary chitchat of fellow passengers. After a halt at the station, the train started moving slowly out of the platform. The pleasure of leaving behind the village to reach the pilgrim centre was clearly visible in the gleaming eyes of Ram Narayan.

The journey to the pilgrim had just started on this delightful note when a young man in a dirty kurta pyjama entered the compartment. He was loaded with an old trunk and a home-stitched cloth bag which had patches on the torn corners. He occupied the seat opposite Ram Narayan's. Discreetly, Ram Narayan frisked the young passenger with his eyes from the side of the newspaper. The short, dark young man wore a big smile that flashed his yellow, betel-stained teeth. His odour was repulsive. He was helping the other passengers in arranging their luggage below the seats. Ram Narayan was not impressed. He could no longer concentrate on his newspaper and ultimately folded it and kept it aside. Now he sat glaring at the unkempt passenger. Whenever their eyes met, the poor young man responded with a gentle smile. But Ram Narayan was clearly quite annoyed with him.

After he sat smiling at Ram Narayan for nearly an hour, in order to strike a conversation, the young man introduced himself as Charan Das. Ram Narayan did not bother to reply, and ignored him. Unembarrassed with the monologue, he continued, "Are you too going on a pilgrimage?" Ram Narayan again ignored his query and started staring out of the window. Every time the youth tried to strike a conversation, Ram Narayan would pretend to be engrossed with either reading his newspaper or sometimes counting his beads. His mind, though, constantly remained focussed on this passenger in front of him. After a couple of hours of the tiring journey, Charan Das opened his tiffin and offered it to Ram Narayan before eating it himself. The air of superiority around Ram Narayan dissuaded him not only from accepting the food but even from thanking the young man for his kind gesture.

After a few minutes, Ram Narayan too felt hungry. He took his neatly wrapped chapatis from the thin cotton cloth and started eating. As soon as he took a couple of bites, the train stopped with a sudden, strong jerk. The food fell on the floor of the train. A disappointed but hungry Ram Narayan did not know how to satiate his hunger pangs. Charan Das could, however, guess it from

his face and immediately took out a packet and offered it to Ram Narayan. For the first time throughout the journey, Ram Narayan responded. He refused to have it on the pretext of not being too hungry. He hoped to buy something from the next station but with the train halting in the middle of nowhere, he did not know how long that would take.

It took several hours for the train to restart. The agitated passengers calmed down and settled in their seats. By this time the sun had already set. Ram Narayan searched for something in his bag, took out a packet of biscuits and ate it to beat his hunger. With the darkness of the night seeping in through the window of the train and the dimming lights, Ram Narayan fell asleep. The night had grown darker and not more than an hour had passed after the train had restarted. It was running at its usual high speed when suddenly the train crumbled and collapsed with a heavy, very heavy judder. Before one could realise what had occurred, the train derailed from its track.

When Ram Narayan woke up, rather, was brought to consciousness, he found himself lying on a hospital bed. He could hardly open his eyes but could hear cries and wails of agony all around. A very few like him were lucky to be alive. Most others lay wrapped in white cloth. Observing a movement in his body, a doctor rushed towards Ram Narayan and asked, "How are you feeling? It's great to see you alive!" Ram Narayan, in his feeble voice asked, "What has happened? Where am I? Have I reached the pilgrim?" He had many more questions to ask but his health and condition did not permit him to talk. The doctor patiently replied, "I'm happy that despite the excessive bleeding you could be saved." Ram Narayan raised his folded hands towards the doctor in a thankful gesture. The doctor immediately responded, "Don't thank me. Thank your son who saved your life. Had he not donated his blood for you, you would not have seen the light of day," explained the doctor. "My son?" Ram Narayan again enquired, as he was completely perplexed. The doctor pointed towards Charan Das lying on the bed next to him, with a swathed head and a plastered leg. "Yes, your son!" confirmed the doctor. Charan Das once again looked at Ram Narayan and flashed a timid yellow smile.

A few days later, upon his recovery, Ram Narayan left for home with a relationship beyond blood, and as a better human being. He had realised that a true pilgrimage was in rising above the mental barriers of class and gentry.

*****

My Little Friend

As a six-year-old with a decaying molar I could easily pass the blame on *mamaji* who got a huge packet of sweets and chocolates everytime he visited us. I hated being forced to brush my teeth. Whenever I was inside the bathroom, I would stand before the mirror and play imaginary games with my toothbrush and the tube of toothpaste. Just to avoid a harsh scolding thereafter, I would rub some water over my lips to convince my mother. But mothers are mothers. Though all children consider themselves smart, I soon realised that all mothers are gifted with a third eye on their forehead and probably a fourth one at the back of their head, carefully concealed in their hair-bun, to keep a thorough check on their children. So I could hardly fool her for 15 minutes, or maybe she pretended to have got fooled before she would drag me to the sink to brush my teeth.

Late one night my decaying tooth started hurting badly. All hell broke loose and my panic-stricken mother left no stone unturned to relieve me of the pain, from calling the dentist, to applying for her own leave, to informing my dad who worked in another state, and then a repeat telecast of all that happened to me to *nani ma*. Next morning, though the pain had subsided temporarily with the painkiller mom gave, the fear of visiting the dentist had not. I was quite reluctant to even step out of the house, but after all, I was still a helpless little boy and could not counter my mother. Though my dentist happened to be a friendly soul, he did not come across as an interesting one. He tried to crack a few jokes to keep me engaged while performing the dental procedure but believe me, those jokes were simply adding on to my annoyance. The only thing that convinced me to forgive him was the reward he promised I would get after I was done with it all. The marbles and kite I would get at the end of the ordeal already made me feel rich, like the owner of some great treasure.

My tooth had decayed considerably and the infection had spread to the adjoining teeth. So I was on an almost regular visit with the dentist at almost the same time slot.

It must have been my third visit and as I exited the clinic with my prized possession tucked safely under my arms, I saw a child about my age standing a few meters away. He looked at me and instantly we exchanged smiles. Childhood actually knows no formalities. You like someone and you acknowledge them with a smile. The boy was in dirty and torn clothes. The buttons of his shirt were hardly in place. His shirt was large enough to have draped two like him. With shabby hair and rough, bare feet, the boy opened his fist to show a small lemon. I too showed him the marbles and kite I had been rewarded with. In no time, we stood face to face and as if we wanted what the other had, without uttering a word, exchanged our prized possessions. There was no question in either of our minds as to who we were, rich or poor, how we knew each other, wrong or right, approval from my mother...not even as to who was likely to be advantageous in the barter. I just knew I had found a new friend with whom I would bond, and we would have a great time together. Our eyes spoke more than our words and our smiles and laughters were the connecting strings that only our hearts could understand.

This continued on every visit of mine to the dentist. My eagerness to go to his clinic started growing as I looked forward to meeting my new friend. Gradually, my dental issues were resolving, and so my almost regular visits now became monthly.

The lemons were precious to me. I would have lemonade made out of those and would safely keep aside the seeds in my pencil box. I planted those seeds in my garden and like a bird waits for its eggs to hatch, I would sit on the garden bench, water them regularly and search every now and then with eagerness to see a sapling.

Two weeks later, on my last visit to the dentist (as my problem was cured), I was desperate to get out of the clinic to meet my friend. Without even waiting to thank the doctor, I ran out. My friend was not there. I went to the gate where I used to meet him but he was nowhere to be seen. My heart filled with disappointment when I saw some stale lemons scattered on the ground. Some were crushed, and some covered with mud. Many had been trampled upon. I could guess my friend had been coming there even when I was not. I was sure that he must have brought all those lemons for me. I picked all the uncrushed lemons and stuffed them into my pocket. There was an unspoken love and feeling of care for him in my heart. He had not stopped bringing me lemons in the hope that I shall turn up some day.

But as the carefree childhood days flew by, I had no regrets but only happiness. Soon, saplings grew from the lemon seeds. Today, after twelve years I have nurtured my friendship

DENTAL
CLINIC

in the form of the lemon tree. Its fruits may be sour and tangy but my love for my childhood friend has grown fonder and sweeter by the years. I hope to meet him again some day!

*****

Grandma Isn't Sleeping!

June was the most awaited month of the year and like every year, my parents had made plans for the vacation with me and my little sister. This year we planned to visit Japan. There was still a week left but the packing and planning had begun. Not a day passed without our visit to the shops to buy clothes for each of us. My sister and I took every advantage of the enthusiasm of our parents to get the best board games and books for our journey. But despite looking forward to visiting exotic places, somewhere deep down my heart I always missed our visits to grandma's house.

My clearest memories of my early childhood are of visiting my grandmother two or three times a year. After dadaji passed away, she lived alone and aloof in her lovely cottage in the hills of Nainital. It was such a beautiful place that I sometimes wondered why we could not live there forever. One could enjoy boating amid the scenic beauty of the hills resting in the enormity of the sparkling lakes. Walking down the illuminated Mall Road, eating ice-creams even in the chilling wind, feeding the ducks in the lake, climbing the sloping entrance to her cottage and then running down, almost sliding. I remember even touching some clouds from her balcony once and pretending to lick them like a cotton candy. It used to be so much fun smoking out our breath as if smoking a cigar, in the freezing nights on the rooftop. The rain would bring even more beauty to the hills as it adorned them with a translucent linen-like white sheet of mist. There was almost everything that I would enjoy, along with that which I could get nowhere else—dadi's love and pampering.

I vividly remember the days when we would visit her. Before our car could reach the gate of her cottage, dadi could be seen waiting eagerly for us. She would not have the patience to wait for the door of the car to open and would herself open it for my sister and me, and hug both of us so tight. I could certainly sense the love and warmth in her hug that was beyond comparison. Our proximity during that hug used to be such that I could nearly smell my favourite *attey ka halwa* prepared by her a short while ago. She would then, allowing both of us to remain clinging to her body, bless my parents who would be touching her feet. Hardly able to walk, she would struggle with all the strength left in her fragile feet to move as fast as she could to serve us refreshments. Though now, considering her old age, dad had kept an attendant to nurse her, dadi would herself do everything to pamper us— from cooking the food, to laying the table, and setting our beds. Dadi would have so many questions about our school, friends, new games, and would hear us even more patiently than my parents would. At night, my sister and I would grab her towards our bed to hear stories from her. Her story bank was truly a treasure box. From her own childhood stories to those of my father, the catena of fables was never-ending. Like a gene from the lamp, she had a story in her kitty on almost any topic we could imagine.

I also remember that dadi looked older with each visit. She would keep coughing intermittently over the phone. I did not exactly know what it meant but could sense that her health was deteriorating.

That year, just three days were left for our

trip, when suddenly, my father got a call from the nurse attending grandma. The call left my father quite shaken which was followed by a night-long discussion over the plan to cancel our planned trip. I was only ten then, but I could sense the gravity of the issue and was absolutely not disappointed about the cancellation of our trip though my sister threw a tantrum till she was tucked into bed. That night, I pretended to sleep to overhear my parents. "She is in coma!" said my father to my mother. They decided we leave for grandma's house the next morning. The bags were already packed but the destination had changed. My mother unpacked some of the toys, and added books, puzzles and crayons to keep us busy. She also put aside our fancy vacation dresses and added some comfortable light woolens. After my first speech in the morning assembly at school a couple of months ago, this was the second time I was in jitters. I was concerned about dadi without even knowing that 'coma' could any time put a 'fullstop' to her life.

I really don't know when I fell asleep that night but when I woke up I was in the car with my family, driving through the hills. We had nearly reached granny's house but for the first time, I did not see her waiting for us at the gate. The gate and the road to her house appeared barren and colourless, as if it were an arid desert. The cool winds blew the drizzles of the onsetting monsoon over my face as I peeped out of the car window. Finally, we were there, but no one was there to warmly embrace us.

As my father honked the car horn to announce our arrival, I saw grandma's house help hurriedly coming out to open the main gate. I was desperately missing the welcoming hugs of my grandma. The old maid served us tea. I was impatient to catch a glimpse of dadi at once. As we entered her room which was strongly smelling of medicines, I saw the growing hopelessness on my father's face.

Soon, he was engrossed in some serious talk about her health and consultations over phone with her doctor. I gently touched her wrinkled hands entangled in glucose drip. The needle of the drip brutally pierced the visible blue veins. I could still feel the warmth and cosiness of her soft hand.

The entire day passed without a caress in my hair, a whisper of surprise in my ear or a snuggly nestle in her lap. By now, I could gather that she was into a deep sleep, perhaps forever, and that horrific thought rolled tears down my eyes as the grim reality began to sink into my heart and mind. I buried my face into the pillow and kept crying the whole afternoon. Each tear that fell down my eye pleaded for her recovery. The food had lost its taste and the water made my throat even more dry. My little sister was indeed in her blissful tender age when one does not understand what it means to almost lose a dear one. Rather, her smiles and naughty giggles enabled me to cling on to the hope of grandma's recovery even in those tough times.

My ears sought affirmation of hope and my eyes questioned the drooped and despairing faces of my parents. *How could they give up so easily?* I thought to myself, recalling the lessons of childhood taught by them, that God answers true prayers and magics do happen.

That night, I urged my parents to let me sleep beside her. I could read the attendant's empathising look, pitying my hope. Before my bed was prepared beside grandma's, for the first time, I saw my father carefully wrap a warm shawl around her head, gently ensuring that the quilt over her did not leave any space for the chilling wind to enter. He glanced around grandma's room, the drip hanging above the corner of her bed, and instructed the attendant to reset it in an hour. For the first time, I saw him ensuring that the windows were tightly shut so that nothing would intrude her peaceful sleep. He ran to the kitchen to fetch a jug of water and put it on the side table like she once used to place in our room, even though he knew fully well that she would not drink a single drop from it. For the first time, I saw him dimming the lights of her room and surrendering his hope to the darkness. Before retiring for the night, he came close to her, touched her feeble feet and needle-ridden hand, planted a kiss on her forehead and left a crying silence behind him. I had never before seen my father like this. I could certainly perceive a swipe of role between the mother and son. But for me, the throttling darkness of the room was scary. Grandma would never have liked to be surrounded by such gloom and melancholy, so I set the curtains apart for the moonlit wonders of heaven to fall inside her room, and allow the twinkling stars to spread their vibrancy. The moon and stars that night spoke of tales of fairyland, just as dadi once used to tell while casting spells of sleep on us.

A soft breeze gently wafted the room through the gap between the window panes, as if singing the same lullaby she once used to sing for us.

My sleep was disturbed by the creek of the door opening. I pretended to be in deep sleep. I knew it was my father peeping to ensure if she was fine. Strange are these sentiments that flash up when we lose or are about to lose a dear one. Perhaps it was just this much that grandma might have craved for, a little love, a little attention, a little care for the child in each one of us. These thoughts kept cropping up till I sunk into a deep sound sleep, till I was again woken up in the middle of the night by a soft pat on my hand. I was astonished to see dadi's hand upon mine. She had indeed moved her fingers. My hope was not a false belief after all! For once, I thought of announcing it to all but then it was better to let grandma relish the

affection that she yearned for in her loneliness. By now I knew that grandma wasn't unaware of our presence. She was aware that her beloved family was with her, and cared for her, and she could peacefully go to sleep.

*****

The Letter Box

The summer sun of June was at its scorching height and the hot winds of the afternoon knocked at my thick-curtained windows. After a long search, I had finally moved into a new rented house which nested in a serene locality away from the din of the bustling city.

Before I could start arranging my stuff, I decided to relax with a cup of tea to boost my energy. As I cleaned the dust over the slab and gas burner to lay my tea pan, I noticed an old man outside my window dragging his feet as he walked, like a reluctant child being compelled to go to school.

I could trace a despairing droop in his shoulders as he reached the rusty letter box at his main gate. The disappointment grew on his face and his wrinkles sagged even more as his hands, trembling with old age, opened the box. Perhaps the letter box was empty, perhaps he was expecting to hear from a loved one. The thoughts kept floating in my mind.

As I finished my cup of tea, I was back to my chores but the woeful eyes of the old man kept striking my head like a bouncing ball. After I was over with all the work, and the room looked more like a human dwelling than a cowshed, I decided to familiarise with the area and went for a walk. The sun was setting and the gleams of blue and orange hues had coloured the sky. I could hear the excited chirps of the birds flying back to their nests. The neighbourhood houses had started being illuminated with the light of bulbs. The blooming jasmines fragranted the lanes.

As I looked at my surroundings with child-like curiosity, I noticed the only unlit house, concealing its presence in the morbid dims of the dying day. I recalled that it was the same house where I had seen the old man and thought he wasn't home, till the creak of the iron gate broke the silence of the evening. He was again there searching the letter box and finding nothing, returned to his confines. The monotony made me curious to know what the old man awaited in the letter box with such desperation. Fortunately, I soon befriended the local sweeper Kishan who showed up every morning, and besides cleaning the lane, sang along with the birds, infusing life into the morning air. He was a nice jolly fellow and seemed much interested in gossip. Perhaps it was therefore that he knew quite a lot about the locality, from who lived where or to some extent, even about the family affairs of each. I could gather this as he had almost investigated into my profile within 15 minutes of conversation.

"Who lives in that house?" I asked Kishan. "Oh, that poor old Bhatnagar Saab..." he replied and without much insistence laid bare his profile too. "He retired a long time ago;had many properties all of which he sold for the education of his only son... and as it usually happens in classic Bollywood movies... the son left him," he exclaimed with a little pretense of sympathy for the old man.

"No one has heard of his son for long now. And after the death of Mrs. Bhatnagar, the old man is all alone. Now every day, he awaits a letter from his son," he answered, almost settling my curiosity. Deep in my heart I sympathised with the old man for we all know how hard our parents strive to raise us and it would be most ungrateful of any child to disappoint the expectations of their parents for their own leisures. The story of the old man compelled me to ponder what I myself had done for my parents. Had I too not been ignoring them for quite long?

My mother calls me every afternoon just to know if I am well. How hurt she must be feeling every time I do not answer her call because of office work. She must be feeling the same as I feel when my six-year-old refuses to talk over telephone saying he is busy assembling his train track toy or watching his favourite cartoon on the T.V. It made me ponder on how casually we take for granted the feelings of our parents and their lifelong selfless efforts struggling to make our lives comfortable which cannot be repaid in any form. I then realised that it was almost two weeks since I had last spoken to my mother. I immediately called her up and relieved myself of this guilt to some extent.

It had been a month of my stay in the

rented house and I was almost adapted to the prosaic episodes of Mr. Bhatnagar waiting for a word of hope from his son. One day, something strange caught my eye. I saw a childlike sparkle in the old man's eyes as he curiously opened the letter box. He now started to frequent it even more and wore a pleasant smile every time like never before. The much-ignored barren garden once again spread the fragrance of wet soil. Its flowers danced to the rhythm of sprinkling water. The little earthen vessel at the entrance gate sparkled with fresh water.

The zeal with which Mr. Bhatnagar would come out of his gate to open the letter box and check something remained a mystery to me. For sure, his son hasn' t started writing to him daily, I said to myself as I never saw him holding a letter as he returned home. Then, what was it that had infused a new life in a dying man as the first showers of the season sprout new hope in the cracked dry earth. There was no end to my curiosity as day by day, I saw a tender smile on his face and his sorrowful eyes light up

with a sparkle. Early one morning, I walked towards the letter box pretending to be taking a morning stroll, with my eyes watchful and alert to see if someone was watching me. Deep inside me was a shameless curiosity to know what was there in the letter box that was making the old man happy. I looked to my left and right ensuring I was out of any surveillance, and as I neared the box, the twitters of nested life grew clear and the twigs lunging out spoke of the tenderness that had sprouted inside. There was a small nest with two nestlings chirping softly as I came closer. Without further disturbing the tiny birds, I left with a teary eye. Surely the old man had found a new life, a new family, a fresh purpose, and indeed one more occasion to shower his selfless concern. In a way I learnt to cherish the beautiful moments with my dear ones and value the small joys that last lifelong.

*****

Who Was That Stranger?

Last year, 16 November was an unusual morning for me as I awoke with the shrill ring of the alarm in my phone. Usually, my sleep would be hampered with the sound of the utensils being washed in the kitchen (which I thought was a deliberate attempt by Shantabai to wake me up). And if that failed, she would leave my room light switched on after cleaning it, till I yelled at her and stuffed my head under the pillow pretending to sleep off again. My mother would then come and sternly order me to get up at once and help her with the household chores. But my pleading look would melt her and she would allow me some more time to sleep.

But some instinct compelled me to pick up the phone that morning.

'We could not save him'. My phone screen flashed with a message from the hospital where my Dad lay battling for life.

It had left me in deep mourning as I knew it was the final nail in the coffin within my heart. Losing my Dad, my pillar of support, had left me heartbroken, numb. *How will I live without him?* was the first thought that entered my mind. My breakup with Ajay had already shattered me. I could not come to terms with the fact that a silly argument could have ended a relationship of five years in a flash.

Dad had become my pillar of strength and solace in those trying months. I had clung to him like a parasite and now he too was gone. *Gone???* Even six months later, that dreadful morning felt like a nightmare. I would often meet Dad in my dreams wanting to hold on to him forever, never letting him go again. I was unable to get over the grief and shock and I spent days and nights mourning my loss.

My Dad, my idol. Though he was a man of strong personality and appeared to be tough, I knew that he was very emotional and kind since the time I secretly saw him shedding tears on the demise of his father, though he would never admit it. He was bright and sharp, but would pretend to give up easily when I put forth my childish riddles. When happy, he would joke around and sing duets with Ma, but when his temper exploded, we would all hide in various corners, waiting for it to subside. I had seen him through my growing years as a highly principled man, with a witty charm and immense love for humanity. He surely was short-tempered but with each passing year, I could sense the mellowness creeping in. In fact, in the last few years before he left us, he was as calm as the morning breeze though he would often succumb to emotional breakdowns whenever he remembered my late grandparents.

Since he was a man of determination and too strong to give up hope... hope to live on... hope to survive, I had thought he would bounce back to health with the strength of his will power. His unexpected demise left a void in my very existence. Moving away from my city was a deliberate attempt to immerse myself into work in my studio, and of course, keep away from memories of Dad. But I would talk to my mother over phone every evening ever since I shifted to Delhi, knowing well how lonely she was without him. However, despite all endeavours, our conversations would always end on a teary note about him.

In my heart I felt that I had no more strength to carry on with my life without Dad. He was my guiding light, my rockstar.

I had no one to share my sorrow with so I

would go to the park in the evening and sit on the bench hidden behind the huge neem tree. I would observe the children playing, hear the merry chirping of birds, meet friendly old people, but nothing would cheer my heart. I confess that I was so deeply depressed that I had begun to think of ending my life. Life seemed like a heavy burden to carry.

It was a Saturday evening but the chill in the air had discouraged people to come to the park, except me who was trying to find solace in the brutal weather. Sitting with my eyes closed with thoughts of the futility of life, I suddenly heard a soft voice in my ear. I opened my eyes and saw an old man sitting next to me. He had dropped his pen and his hands were trembling. I bent and returned his pen and he thanked me profusely. Though he must have clearly guessed my lack of interest in holding any conversation with him, he started telling me why the pen was so precious to him. He said, "I had bought it to gift it to my daughter a year ago before she relocated to her own world."

"Her own world?" I questioned with curiosity.

"Oh! Another country, quite far from here... practically a different world from mine," he answered.

I felt a certain bonding with him. After that day, we would meet daily on the bench hidden behind the huge neem tree.

He would talk about his daughter with great fondness, and with a smile. He told me how he had embraced her in his arms as a new born to how she grew up into an independent teenager. I was bemused that not a single drop of tear ever rolled down his eyes nor did his voice tremble as he recalled her memories.

One evening I questioned, "Don't you miss her?" He simply smiled and politely answered that he tries finding her in me and therefore comes to meet me in the park. Then the old gentleman got up from the bench and left. I started finding myself to be relevant to someone.

As the days passed, our friendship grew and I began to have an emotional connect with him. He introduced himself as Ratna Sagar and told me that he lived nearby in house number 384 of the society. Association with the old man changed my perspective towards my own life. It struck a positive change in me just as a caterpillar must feel while transforming into a butterfly.

I too told him about my father and how I missed him. One day in a conversation with him I expressed how I strongly disapproved his daughter's decision to pursue her own dreams, leaving him all alone. For me, it was indeed selfish of her to do that to her father. Mr Ratna Sagar looked at me, smiled and asked, "Is it not what all daughters do?" His query left me pondering over my own decision to leave

my mother behind. *Wasn't I too being selfish in thinking only about my sorrows so far?* I deeply introspected through the night sitting under the dim table lamp on my study table.

I do not recall when I slipped into deep sleep. I was woken up by the ringing of the doorbell. I opened the gate to find a little gift placed nicely on the mat. Surprised, I carefully picked it up. It was a surprise birthday gift from Mr Ratna Sagar. I must have told him of my birthday in some conversation which I did not remember now. I opened the box to find a 'precious' pen inside. I recalled it was the same pen that Mr Ratna Sagar had bought for his daughter. *But why would he gift it to me?* I thought. I anyway, decided to walk down his house to at least thank him. I rang the bell of his house and waited for him to open the door. A young man in his mid-thirties opened the gate and asked, "Yes?"

I was confused by the presence of the young man in the house but answered, "Mr Ratna

Sagar....I had come to thank him for the gift." With a puzzled expression, the young man said that no man named Ratna Sagar has ever lived in that house. Before I could gather my wits, my phone rang. Of course, it was my mother calling to wish me. Her speech was hesitant and her words minced.She kept apologising without lifting the shroud of suspense. "What's the matter, Ma?" I asked patiently calming her.

I could not believe my ears when she told me that she had misplaced the precious pen that Dad had bought for me to gift me on my birthday. I realised that the pen I was holding in my hand right now was indeed a special gift from my father through an unknown stranger.

I am now assured in my newfound belief that after leaving his mortal coil, Dad has started residing in my heart and soul, and thus is always near me.

*****

My First Date

Having completed my graduation in law almost thirteen years ago with a gold medal had certainly paid me well. While at my age, my father had been struggling to secure a decent life for us, I was already crafting my own path to fortune. Being one of the top heads of my litigation firm, life was rushing at the speed of a bullet train. No time to relax, no time to look back, no time to hold on, or I may say, there were no commas or fullstops. I missed the time when I last sipped my coffee leisurely breathing in its aroma. Perhaps this fast paced lifestyle was the reason I was still single at the age of 37! But no regrets. After all, I had everything any young legal entrepreneur could not even dream of—a lucrative job, spacious bungalow, luxury cars, servants attending you day and night, reputation, status, bla bla…I owed it all to a strictly disciplined lifestyle.

It was nine in the morning of a heavily rainy day of July. One could gauge the mood of the weather even without gazing through the window. The message of my cook being on leave flashed on my phone. Shambhu, my home-manager-cum-driver was also late by a good 35 minutes by now. I was a stringent boss in allowing any leverage to such delays. I called him up. My ungentle speech was marked by harsh words and a raging temper, warning to dismiss him from service. I may have given him similar warnings a thousand times earlier, but my dependence on him for so long prevented me from executing my threats. He had been with me for almost five years now so certainly no one else could have managed my household affairs better than him. With time, Shambhu had remarkably mastered the art of resilience towards my attitude. With no other lucrative job opportunities available to him, the poor fellow couldn't afford to leave his position at my place. My yellings had made him stubborn and thick-skinned now. He threw punctuality to the winds and was ready with all sorts of lame excuses for an unpredictable leave or turning up late. The monsoon season furnished him with innovative excuses of being late, such as his bike breaking down due to water logging on the streets, could not inform prior as there were no signals, having missed a bus, or bus being over-crowded, etc.

Today was a slightly off-the-normal-schedule day for me. My parents who lived in Bangalore had finally succeeded in convincing me to bind myself in nuptials. They had found a suitable match for me in my own city, Delhi. Ritu apparently was a perfect match for me.

Only a working woman like her, I believed, would have understood my time limitations and work restrictions. So far, we had talked once or twice over the phone and, upon her insistence, I agreed to meet her. So technically, it was going to be my first date.

I had never thought that going on a date could be so nerve-racking. For a confident and well-read advocate like me who had fought fierce legal battles, it was an alien feeling. Without wasting much time, I gulped my coffee and got ready in the most sophisticated and elegant attire, to impress Ritu. Pretty confident of my looks, I intended to showcase my opulence but Shambhu had already ruined it partially. *Now I will have to drive by myself in the rain!* I thought to myself in disgust.

So here I was, a brilliant top-notch lawyer, partially starved, ready to drive through a clogged city to meet his first date. I had so far hardly reached half the route, and was disgusted to see the cars and vehicles lined up in the heaviest traffic of the decade. The road was mercilessly flooded with rain water and people were crazily honking their car horns. The deafening cacophony was playing on my eardrums. For twenty minutes my car didn't budge a centimeter. It was such a waste of time to merely gaze outside your car window to see the city floating. Just then, I noticed some children, perhaps from the nearby slum or may be living on the streets, enjoying the muddy waters, splashing and pouncing in the pool created by nature. For a moment their ecstasy and joy made me forget the annoyance of the traffic. Thankfully, after a long wait, the traffic started inching but as I turned on my car, it did not start. I repeatedly tried but the engine had stopped working. It kept making a stern sound as if yelling back at me like I had...at Shambu. Perhaps some power was trying to make me realise that yes, cars and bikes do break down in waterlogged streets.

I had no option but to push my car to the side of the road. I carefully removed my expensive clothes, and kept them on the back seat. I feared that the heavy rain would drench and spoil them. I came out of the car to push it. The rain fell with full force all over me, thumping and whipping my back, banishing its elegance and sophistication. It was a great surprise to me to see a few men in their shabby clothes come out to help me push my car to the other side. None of the elite bothered to step out of their pompous vehicles to help a stranded soul in the middle of a flooded road. These strangers living on the streets, the slumdwellers, not just moved my car to the other side, they moved my very heart and soul. They also forced me to reconsider what I had thought of them so far. It wasn't just my vehicle that had broken that day, it was also the illusionary castle of superiority and arrogance that the rain broke within me. I was deeply touched by the gesture of these men whom I considered menial and subjugating for money. I was at a loss of words to thank them. The rain was incessantly falling and I had no option but to take shelter beneath an overcrowded bus stand. I tried calling for help from the office but there was no signal in the phone. I decided to travel by bus.

A bus finally came after a fifteen-minute wait but the crowd pushed me back, making it impossible for me to edge towards it. Of course, I missed it! Every other bus that came was so overloaded with people and stuffed beyond capacity that it appeared that the entire town was packed inside it. Every minute that passed mocked my pledge of punctuality. I then decided to walk towards my destination. With this decision, I was sure to have to bid adieu to my elegant Charles and Keith shoes forever. As my feet immersed in the puddle, I heard a few street children chuckling at me. One of them laughed and demonstrated how it should be done. He suddenly jumped barefoot in the logged water from above a short height and continued to splash and jump till he thought he had taught me enough of the art. Soon, some more friends of that fun-loving urchin joined the race to train me in that art of jumping into the puddle. Their giggles and joyous laughters cast a spell over me to join them. Those splashes made me forget all tensions of life, and as I jumped up and down I realised that life can never be caged in discipline. Maybe, the bouncing and the ups and downs are the true discipline of life. I was out of my golden shelter, amid nature.I had given up on my luxurious car and worn off my sophistication and monotony, to catch on the liveliness of life.

I realised how often people whom we look

down upon, can be the most important ones in your life; how we sometimes choose to ignore the unprivileged merely because we are blessed with luxuries. I was glad to have had the most important, and the very first date with my own self that day.

*****

An Inauspicious Day

It had taken a couple of years for Muhammad Abdullah to reconcile to the fact that he was no longer capable of carrying his lineage of tailoring forward. Cataract had blurred his vision and therefore, his efficacy to continue stitching. This was what prompted Abdullah to surrender his 'Master ji' title.

To make matters worse, his reluctant son Zahid was very critical and highly embarrassed to inherit the tailoring profession. He had gone to pursue further studies in the nearby town after finishing his middle schooling in the village with fair grades. He was eager to leave the village life behind and move ahead in life, so that he would not be compelled to remain stuck in the profession of his forefathers. Though he had been a just average student so far, the education system had at least pulled him out of the orthodox mindset so deep-rooted in his aging father.

An astrologer had recently predicted that his son would die very soon, which put Abdullah on tenterhooks. He tried to call his son back from the town, accusing him of being irresponsible towards his parents but his pleas fell on deaf ears. Thereafter, despite a poor telephonic connectivity in the village, Abdullah made it a point to remain in touch with his son every day. For that, he would keep waiting for hours before his son called him from an STD booth.

Today was a usual day for all but for Abdullah, whose peaceful sleep had been interrupted by a nightmare last night. He woke up sweating heavily, and with a limping leg and a hazy eye, he ran towards the old wall clock. It was 5:15 am and the day had just started to dawn. Rubbing his eyes again, he tried taking a clearer note of the time. He was still breathing heavily. *A morning dream is always true*, thought a nervous Abdullah to himself as he swiftly walked to wake up his wife. She tried to pacify him, and gave him a glass of water but Abdullah was firm in his belief that something inauspicious was about to happen. In a trembling voice Abdullah blurted out to his wife, "I saw Zahid dying!" His eyes were as teary as his throat was dry. The nightmare of his son's demise, that too, at the crack of dawn was enough to convince him that it was indeed true.

Hours passed but his anxiety did not abate. Abdullah still seemed lost in the dreadful thought when his wife came and quietly gave him a glass of tea. As it was bound to happen for a man lost in his irrational grief, Abdullah accidentally struck the table and the glass of tea tumbled to the ground and broke. "Allah!" Abdullah pleaded mercy as it was yet another bad omen. His fear was strengthening and he was certain of the impending doom.

His wife could sense the growing anxiety in Abdullah but could not do anything to remove the thought from his mind, the seeds of which had been planted by his astrologer friend. Abdullah did not have the patience to wait till evening for his son's call so he decided he would himself call him from the STD booth which was hardly any distance for a healthy, sturdy person, but for an aging Abdullah it was tiresome and painful for his weak joints. Undeterred by the scorching heat of the summer sun that pierced through his body, Abdullah walked till he was jolted with another inauspicious sign, as if the two earlier signs that morning, i.e., the nightmare and then the breaking of the glass of tea were not enough to rattle him completely. "Allah!" Abdullah again cried for mercy as he saw a sneaky black cat crossing his path as swiftly as it could, not the least aware that it had caused a bad omen for the old man. But of course, Abdullah did not dare to walk further till a bullock cart passed by. Finally, after a few hours, he reached the STD booth only to be told that the phone was not working since morning. A disappointed Abdullah had no option but to pray to the Almighty to prevent the inauspicious. As he was returning home, the postman excitedly called out to him, "Masterji! a telegram for you!" Stopping his bicycle near him, he pulled out the bundle of telegrams and took out the one addressed to Abdullah. He intentionally chose to wait there while Abdullah opened the telegram, expecting some money for reading it out to him. For the inauspicious happenings since morning, Abdullah was rather apprehensive and with trembling hands returned it to the postman to hear what it read. "Son passed. Was sick too", read the message.

Abdullah's eyes pleaded to the postman to translate the message but the greedy postman pretended to be in a hurry to deliver other letters, expecting a few more coins in his pocket. Without wasting time, an anxious Abdullah took out a five-rupee note from his pocket, pleading with the postman to translate the message. Before the postman could utter a word, Abdullah confirmed "Is it from my son?" The postman examined the telegram from all notches and corners and replied, "Not exactly from your son. Someone seems to have sent it on his behalf. It says he has passed. But wait, he was sick too. Maybe he has......" The postman wore a sombre expression. "What do you mean?" Abdullah almost screamed at him.

"Passed could also mean he is no more!" the postman, no great scholar of English himself, said in a low voice.

Abdullah's legs crumbled down in shock, rendering him almost pale and lifeless. His tears rolled down his cheeks and he cried his heart out in grief.

The postman condoled him and dropped him to his house on his bicycle. The news spread like wildfire and soon, the lonely house saw a gathering of relatives, friends and neighbours grieving over the death of the young lad.

A little later, entered the schoolmaster of the local school where Zahid had studied till class eight. Everyone in the gathering rose up for him respectfully. After all, he was the most educated man in the entire village. He gently sat down next to Abdullah to share his grief. A grieving Abdullah passed the telegram to the schoolmaster crying, "Look, what has happened!"

The schoolmaster carefully took the paper and read it. He again read it to himself but seemed to be confused a bit.

"Where does it say that your son has.... I mean, died?" he asked, scratching his head. The schoolmaster seemed perplexed and found it awkward and challenging to even convince Abdullah that the words in the telegram could mean something else. But Abdullah was certain that his nightmare had come true, considering the one after the other ill-omens he had encountered during the day. The schoolmaster tried to convince him to believe that the letter had been misread and misinterpretted. So, like an investigating officer he questioned Abdullah, "Did Zahid appear in the annual examinations recently?"

A still hopeless Abdullah replied, "Yes...a few days ago.... But what's the use now? He has left us all!" he bawled.

The schoolmaster forced him to once again try calling his son. Abdullah realised that the hope came from a literate mind so he agreed without resistance.

The schoolmaster took Abdullah to his house which was the only one in the village with a telephone. All the friends, and relatives, along with his wailing wife, followed them. Abdullah handed over the phone number of the hostel from where his son used to call, to the school master and stood with folded hands and pleading eyes. His heart was beating fast as the schoolmaster dialled the number. He could hear the phone ringing at the other end. Abdullah heard the schoolmaster converse with the person at the other end but did not have the courage to interrupt. His eyes had a thousand questions as the schoolmaster kept down the phone.

The smile of the school master said it all. "He who believes in superstition must believe in miracles," he said, laughing heartily and patting a much-relieved Abdullah's shoulder. "Your son has passed his exam but could not call you as he was sick so he asked a friend from

the hostel to send you a telegram to convey the good news," the schoolmaster informed him. "His warden has promised that he will make your son talk to you tomorrow."

The schoolmaster explained to Abdullah how the negative beliefs in superstitions had taken over his mind in such a way that it refused to believe anything else.

Like Abdullah we all are often surrounded by our own myths and beliefs which cast an invisible veil over our rational thought process. That night, Abdullah slept soundly and promised to himself that he won't be superstitious anymore.

*****

A Wish

Somewhere in a congested slum of Mumbai, Radha Bai (a migrant from Bihar) had been fighting against odds single-handedly after the demise of her husband. Though Radha was up the creek without a paddle to educate and raise her only son, she was determined to provide him the best possible life. From her patched and faded cotton saree, to her ill-fitting rubber footwear, all spoke of her misery and hardships. When her husband died, she had flatly refused to take off her *mangalsutra* and her *bindi* from her forehead. She felt closer and connected to her husband through the black and golden beads hanging close to her heart, and also through her maroon bindi. Apart from the mangalsutra and the conspicuous bindi, the most precious vestige of her deceased husband was their only son, Raju.

One Friday afternoon, Raju barged in, banging the dilapidated door against the unpainted cemented wall. He threw his schoolbag on the floor and demanded water from Kamla Tai, their neighbour, who took care of him while Radha went out for work. "Wait, I will give you water son," said a faint and feeble voice from the cot. A concerned Raju was surprised to find his mother at home at that hour. She was lying on the cot, struggling to get up to fetch water for him. As he held her, he realised she had high fever. Her hands were burning hot like the chapati she served him for dinner. "You didn't go for work, aayi?" he asked, concerned about the health of his mother, but equally worried about the pay deduction that would result from her leave.

The disappointment on his face spoke more than his words as he sipped the water.

Radha sat beside him. She could read his thoughts. She said, “Don’t worry, dear. Everything will be fine one day. Things will certainly improve.” Annoyed with the circumstances and feeling helpless, Raju covered his face with his hands and started sobbing. Radha embraced the boy and caressed his hair to calm him. She tried to divert his anxiety by asking about his day at school. “Today my teacher told us a story of the wishing coin. You just make a wish, keep a coin by your bed and if the coin vanishes, your wish comes true....Aayi, I am fed up of such false tales. I know we are always going to remain like this!” the dejected boy said. Radha softly patted his back in reassurance of her promise and tried convincing her son not to lose hope when in her heart, she herself saw darkness all around.

From his pending school fee, to the unpaid rent, her increasing debts were throttling her. She made every effort to conceal her worries from her son but the leaking roof and the empty flour-tin announced it aloud. "I well know that I cannot afford new school shoes like Sunil or go out for a movie like many of my friends. I am bullied and teased for our poverty. Even Shyam the backbencher who never studies and always fails, gets a whopping pocket money of hundred rupees a month... but I get only a one-rupee coin each day as if I can buy a bungalow out of it," complained Raju. Poor Radha had no answer to his questions. She doubted if she would ever be able to meet his expectations. With each expectation of Raju, the void of her husband grew wider within her.

Radha gently calmed him and said, "The story is indeed true. I am sure one day God will grant more than you wish for after he has fulfilled the wishes of your privileged friends." She took out a shiny one rupee coin from her worn out purse and gave it to Raju, asking him to try the magic tonight though herself she was unsure if she would be able to meet the wish or fit into God's shoes.

Raju excitedly took out a paper chit from his bag, scribbled something and secretly folded it back. He then kept it with the coin that Radha had offered him and buried it under his pillow. As Raju slept soundly, Radha decided to see for herself what he had wished for. She would try to fulfil that wish for her dear little boy. As she read the wish, the chit suddenly appeared very heavy in her hands. Raju badly wanted a bicycle. Though it appeared impossible, for Radha it was an opportunity to instill hope in her son.

The next morning, Raju got up and rushed outside to see if his wish was fulfilled. His eager eyes searched every nook and corner outside his house but was left disappointed when he found no bicycle. Knowing what Raju was looking for, Radha asked him to patiently wait till sunset. "God must be busy with other children's wish lists too. Be patient and wait till sunset," Radha calmed a disappointed Raju.

Her fever had subsided by now. As she prepared to leave for work, she asked Raju to get ready for school as Kamla Tai entered the cottage. Radha greeted her and left. Sitting in the bus to her employer's house, her attention was drawn to the cyclists on the road and the cycle shop hoardings. Her eyes silently searched for one for her son. Even after she reached the house where she worked as a maid, her eyes kept darting towards the cycle of the houseowner's daughter parked in the portico. Pinki was almost the same age as Raju. She was an affectionate girl but possessive about her belongings. *Pinki baby would never agree to give away her cycle,* Radha thought to herself.

This was her only hope to get her son a cycle. Like everyday, Pinky came to Radha to seek the candy that Radha would unforgettably ensure to carry, to please the little girl. She let Pinki frisk her bag but there was none today. The girl then frisked Radha's purse to check but could not lay her hands on anything except two crumpled currency notes and the paper chit. Radha apologised to Pinki and promised two candies the next day and silently proceeded with the pending chores. Every cycle bell that she heard from outside the window reminded her of an unfulfilled promise which seemed a farfetched dream. The cycle ring of the children of the locality racing on their tiny bikes and their giggles echoing through the window above the kitchen sink distracted her mind as she washed the utensils.

She then decided to seek help from Pinky's mother though she was convinced of a refusal as she had already taken an advance salary for the next month. But her motherly love prompted her to try at least. She hesitantly went to her and softly implored, "Madam ji, if you ever plan to sell Pinky baby's cycle..." Before the mistress could utter anything, her expressions said it all. Her brows frowned in annoyance but before her denial could find a word, Pinki intervened to request her mother to buy her a new cycle. "Mama, you know how old my cycle is now. I need to have a new one anyway. Please Mama, buy me a new one. Please! Pleeeeeeaaaase! Puhleeeeeaaase!" Pinki implored as only kids can to melt their mother's heart. The mistress could do nothing but to give in to her daughter's request to buy her a new cycle, and so allowed Radha to take the old one.

Radha turned towards Pinki with gratitude. Her eyes were teary and she was at a loss for words but her silent lips and melting heart thanked her. The girl, perhaps, had read the chit when she frisked Radha's bag, vetting a candy for herself.

Radha completed all her work and hurried home with the cycle, so fast that the 4-km walk ended sooner than the bus travel. She quietly parked the cycle outside and pretended to be unaware of anything as she entered the house in her usual manner. She saw Raju doing his homework and deliberately teased him. "So what happened to your wish?" Raju looked at her sadly and turned his disappointed face back to his worksheet. On Radha's persuasion, Raju got up to check outside the house. As soon as he saw the cycle, he started jumping in excitement and hugged Radha. At that moment, there could be nothing more satiating for Radha than being embraced by her son.

A few days later, Raju again sought a coin from Radha and wrote a wish on the slip. This time it was for a school bag. The wish wasn't at all over-demanding. Raju's old bag was badly torn. Its shredded corners made way for the books to peep out, and enough space for small articles to slide off. It was no longer able to hold the pressure of the heavy books. Its outer pocket had become useless with the broken zip. Pinki's Mom had no objection in donating the used bag of her daughter. Radha could somehow also fulfill this second wish of her son but in her heart she began to worry about how she would fulfil his such frequent demands.

A few months later, a new wish cropped up from under his pillow. This time he had demanded a football. Raju had fast learnt to slip a tiny piece of paper under his pillow. "You cannot keep on placing such wishes limitlessly Raju!" exclaimed Radha as she pulled her bag away from Raju in frustration. Raju did not say anything. Probably he realised how precious even a one-rupee coin was for their survival. He silently crushed the small piece of paper in his hand, threw it, and went to sleep. Radha picked up the paper to read what his wish was this time. Her tears fell in ecstasy and pride as she read her son's childish scribbling, informing God that he had been chosen for a football championship by the school and he needed a football to practise. But her joy was short-lived as she remembered the pile of debt that she was burdened with. She was refused an extra penny from anywhere and everywhere. Having no other option to prevent her son's dream from crumbling in the crushed bit of paper in her hand, she decided to sell off her mangalsutra, the precious souvenier of her husband.

The next morning, Radha removed it from her neck and tied it at the end of her saree in a knot. The skies shed heavy tears of rain as if trying to prevent her from selling the only possession of her husband. The seeping raindrops from the holes of a torn out umbrella kept washing her teary eyes but could not wither away her determination to give her son everything that her husband, if alive, would have given.

Raju returned from school. He was excited and over-delighted to see the football on the table tightly wrapped in a polythene.He looked back at his mother and tightly hugged her. His mother's eyes were glimmering in pride but he could sense a void as if her smile stretched a little less, the beat of her heart seemed a bit heavy and her breath a bit hollow. Something seemed missing from her true self. Radha avoided Raju's curious gaze and turned around to hide her tears. She hurriedly pulled out the jute bag hanging behind the kitchen door and left the house to buy vegetables. After selecting a few vegetables she realised that she had forgotten to carry her purse containing money, pending bills, debit receipts, jeweller's slip of the sold mangalsutra, and of course, the wishing slips. She urgently returned home to pick it up. As she entered her house, she realised her son was not there. The slips her son wrote were scattered on the floor and the earthen piggy bank lay broken on the ground. This was the money they had prudently saved over the years and left untouched for a rainy day. He had left another message which read, *My last wish...I wish I could be a better son.* Shocked, Radha's legs turned weak, and her hands trembled, as she stared at the slip of paper with the last message of her son. She felt helpless and defeated as she crumbled in a heap to the ground. Her hopes were finally crushed as she felt she had failed to parent her son alone. She could not withstand her son's growing needs. The sun had set and a blanket of darkness covered the entire house. Radha sat listlessly leaning against the cemented wall, staring into blank space.

Suddenly, the creaking of the wooden door punctuated the silence of the dark room. Someone turned on the lights. It was Raju. "Aayi, what are you doing there?" he exclaimed in concern. He lifted Radha in his arms and

carried her to the cot. He put his hand in his pocket and pulled out his fist. He opened it to surprise his mother. Radha could not stop her tears as she saw her mangalsutra in his palm. The mother and son embraced each other.

Their tears spoke the tale of love and respect for each other's feelings. The leaves seemed to be clapping in the wind, and dripped tears of joy in the rain. Wet leaves of the trees seemed to be shedding tears of joy for an unbound love.

*****

An American Dream

It was half an hour past midnight and the small town of Sunam in Punjab was already draped under the deep slumber of the moonlit night. The windows of a house, however, watched over the dark, murky streets with its faint orange bulb light. Arvind was yet to call it a day till the battery of his laptop survived. It had been a busy day and a busier night for him. Arvind was working on his laptop. His mother was in the kitchen at this late hour. She knew all about the late night hunger pangs of her son. Today, Arvind had outrageously breached the bedtime of the house and his father, a retired bank official who was very particular about time schedules, would have been very upset with Arvind, had he been awake. Mother knocked on Arvind's door and without waiting for his answer, barged inside with a glass of milk. For the Punjabi family, knocking never meant seeking permission to enter, rather a warning, *I am entering!* She placed the glass of hot milk right next to the laptop, commanded Arvind to finish it before going to sleep, and left the room. She knew exactly why Arvind was in front of his laptop at that hour. He had applied for a job in America and was waiting for the selection result. Before his mother could remind him of the unfinished glass of milk, Arvind came out of his room in excitement and tightly embraced his mother. "I got it, Mumma! I got it !" His mother's eyes turned wet in mixed emotions of joy that her son had finally achieved his dream and of the grief of impending separation. She tightly hugged her son and showered her blessings on him.

Soon Arvind's phone started ringing with congratulatory phone calls from friends and colleagues. His mother stood smiling beside the untouched glass of milk. The night was no more dull or dark.

The news spread like wildfire and saw everyone, from the milkman to the grocery store owner, from neighbours and relatives to every local person, greeting and congratulating Arvind. Though there were many young boys in the city who had made it to the U.S. before, it was always a celebratory event to bid a grand farewell to every new boy departing from India. This was perhaps, because none of them so far was ever heard to return before at least five or seven years, or never.

The formalities for departing for the U.S. were to take another one month. Arvind waited impatiently for D-day but his parents felt the clock was ticking too fast. As the day of his departure drew near, the kids of the locality started gathering at the gate of his house in awe to have a glimpse of Arvind everytime he left for office where he was serving his notice period. The barber did not charge him a penny for the special hair cut, shave and facial, as it was indeed the last one at his hometown. The aunties of the neighbourhood brought woolen scarfs and tiffins full of home-made *pinnis* (laddoos) for Arvind on the day when he was set to leave for the airport.

Arvind's Dad was a quiet man. He hardly displayed his affection for his son as his mother would, but while travelling to the Delhi Airport, he held his son's hand. Arvind could feel the warmth of both his parents sitting beside him but none uttered a word. Their hearts were heavy and their throats were dry. Mother preferred to look outside the window most of the time hiding her pain, till she burst into tears at the airport. Her tear-soaked wet dupatta spoke more than she could, while it was the tightest hug that his father ever gave him. All the three were still preparing for the reality to sink in that they would now not be seeing each other for the next five years. This was certainly not a matter of choice but a condition of the employment offer. The old parents stood gazing at the departure gate of the airport till their son disappeared in the crowd inside.

After approximately a 28-hour flight Arvind reached the land of his dreams, New York, U.S. He gazed at the skyline in wonder and was mesmerised by the beauty of the city. The room he lodged in was finer than any hotel in India he had been to so far. He had to report to the office on the same day, so, all dressed up in the new suit and tie with shining shoes, he entered his workplace. He felt rather embarrassed when he saw his colleagues dressed casually in their jackets, jeans and sports shoes. He greeted them but busy in their work, none responded. He quietly took his seat and started to work. All of a sudden, all the employees got up mechanically, and like robots, hustled out of the office. No one informed him that it was a lunch break. But Arvind was carrying his tiffin with aloo parathas and mango pickle lovingly packed by his mother, and the packet of pinnis (laddoos). He was hungry but confused if he could eat it at the office, so he carried his tiffin out, and found a bench for himself. Everyone had burgers and coffee cups with them. He barely had a few bites of the pinni when he saw the employees returning to their cabins. Arvind also hurriedly closed his tiffin and followed them. In the hustle and bustle of the first day at the office, he even forgot to call his parents to assure them that he had reached safely. His phone had two missed calls from home to remind him of that. He immediately left his seat to call back home. He was not only separated by distance but also by time. It was

2 am in India. The father, otherwise punctual about his bedtime, was wide awake and picked up Arvind's call at the first ring. Both the parents were desperately waiting to hear from their son.

Arvind soon adjusted and got used to the American lifestyle. Everytime he prepared an omelette, toast and coffee for himself for breakfast, he reminisced about the hot parathas loaded with homemade ghee and butter that his mother cooked for him. Coffee was quite foreign to their kitchen while a sugar-loaded tea was a staple drink after food. After experimenting with the kitchen utensils and burnt toasts for a while, Arvind had now learnt the art of cooking, though he had not excelled it like a chef.

The lunches and dinners were now ready-to-eat frozen foods. Burgers and cold drinks which could never make their mark in the town of Sunam, were staples for survival.

With packaged milk, there could be no more arguments on the milkman adding water.

Working late at night in America, Arvind would often hallucinate about a knock at his door with his mother about to barge in with a glass of hot milk. His room was no more the only room to be lit at nights as the entire city sparkled in glamour and opulence. Arvind's ears missed the chitchatting of the neighbouring aunties and the giggles of children. No one in America enjoyed the winter sun as much as the octagenarian dadis and dadas back home on their *munjas* (cots) outside their houses. From grocery to vegetable doorstep services of the small town, to the *tring-tring* sounds of the cycle bells and window smashing by the children playing cricket in the open streets, Arvind started longing for India like never before.

Every phone call to his parents reignited this longing but the busy work schedules had indeed affected the frequency of his calls home. Despite that, his mother always sat next to the phone at the scheduled time waiting to hear her son's voice. Arvind had a lucrative job, an income in dollars, but he had no one except himself to spend on. By the end of six months, he had made a few friends, but not one was as close to him as Birju and Lucky, his childhood buddies back home. He often remembered those golden days with them when their lunch or dinner would be at the house of the one whose mother had cooked a tastier dish. Each other's clothes were taken without asking and remained in possession until the rightful owner demanded them back. Arvind was not just a friend to them, but also their teacher in times of crises, such as examinations. They were literally brothers from different mothers.

Unlike in India, the gathering with friends in America was more of a formal affair. One such outing happened on a Sunday night.

The next morning, Arvind woke up vomiting profusely. He tried calling his office friends but none responded to the calls. Arvind's health did not permit him to attend office the next day. The continuous vomiting left him so weak that he fainted in the room. When he gained consciousness after a while, he called the ambulance. He was taken to the hospital and treated. There were doctors and nurses around him but he missed his concerned mother who would have sat next to him putting ice packs on his forehead, or his father who would be enquiring about his health after every five minutes, or his friends rushing to procure medicines.

In the American hospital, Arvind was merely one of the numerous patients. Just then, it struck him. *What if at anytime my parents are in need of medical help?* Arvind's own condition left him so concerned about his aged parents that he decided to leave his job in America and return to India.

A week later, discharged from the hospital, Arvind resigned from the job, served the notice period, and left for India. When he reached his hometown, he found his house locked. It was 3 am and the American instinct (now infused in him to some extent) dissuaded him from disturbing or calling anyone at that hour. *Why would the house be locked?* Shuddering with a qualm of the unforeseen, Arvind kept strolling outside the house in anxiety like a maniac, waiting for the sun to rise. It gave him immense relief when he heard the clinking milk cans. It was the milkman but the only information he had was that the house had remained locked for the last two days. Arvind's heart started sinking with dreadful thoughts. He kept blaming himself for leaving his parents alone in this phase of their lives. A perplexed Arvind could not think of anything but the apprehension of some mishappening.

It then struck him. *Why not call Birju or Lucky?* He called Birju who immediately picked his call. He informed that Arvind's mother was hospitalised due to food poisoning. Arvind urgently rushed to the hospital and met his parents. His mother was recovering well. Birju apologised for not having informed him as his parents did not want to distress him.

Arvind had finally reunited with his parents in his motherland. The sun seemed warmer than before, the breeze was soothing, and the dust of the motherland was indeed more aromatic than ever.

*****

The Untaught Lesson

Though it was already middle of the school session, it was Nitya's first day in her new school. The sudden demise of her parents had changed her life drastically. One such change was her admission to a local public school near her uncle's house. Six-year-old Nitya had matured beyond her age and understanding in barely a few weeks of losing both her parents. She remained impassive to the pretentious display of sympathy by relatives and friends. Her uncle and aunt were now her only solace and refuge. As her guardians, they were caring and affectionate but still incapable of filling the void left in her life by the untimely death of her parents. With a shoestring budget and responsibility towards their own two daughters, it was genuinely difficult for them to provide Nitya the pampered life of a single child which she had so far enjoyed, but was now brutally deprived of. Despite a passive resistance from their two young daughters, Nitya's uncle and aunt adjusted Nitya in the girls' bedroom on a single mattress in a corner. By now, Nitya had learnt the art of endurance and tolerance despite sensing the dislike for her by her cousins.

The ringing schoolbell was suppressed in the indistinct chatters of the students. Nitya sat alone on her seat observing the happiness all around her but within herself, her heart sobbed. A pindrop silence broke the jabbering as Ms. Handa, a strong built, confident lady dressed up neatly in a saree, with her hair tightly tied in a bun, entered the class. The class stood up and greeted her in chorus. The big, black, round bindi on her forehead was as commanding as her authoritative personality. She was the headmistress of the school and was known for her strict nature and strong belief in adhering to the rules of the school. Her big *kohl* eyes peeped above her glasses as she scrutinised and captured the slightest movement of indiscipline in the class. In her heavy voice, she introduced Nitya as the new entrant to the class, preached the values of the school, and instructed the students to adhere to the school timings as well as to remain in proper uniform. The class sighed in relief as she left the classroom.

After the morning prayers, the classteacher Ms. Sonika, a young lady, proceeded with the studies. Time passed by and the school bell announced the closing of the day. The distance from the school to her uncle's house was barely a kilometer, and so Nitya walked to school and back to the house.

One day, Nitya reached school late. Her left sock was also missing. The class teacher looked at her watch and gave her a stern look. She reprimanded her for being late and warned her not to repeat it. Despite the scolding, Nitya appeared happier than before. She had a subtle smile on her lips and her eyes sparkled with joy as if she had discovered a treasure. She calmly sat with her eyes glued to the blackboard but seemed to be lost in her own thoughts. "Nitya, answer this!" said the teacher, waking her from her daydream. Nitya could not understand the disruption and failed to answer the query. What followed was much expected...to stand in punishment outside the class. The only fear was the wrath of the headmistress who often took a surprise round of the school. She was not one to spare an indisciplined child.

As destiny would have it, Ms. Handa found her prey for the day. Her harsh, heavy words fell on Nitya's ears but not on her mind. The

feeble child stood silently with hands up and a smile on her face. till Ms. Handa left and she was allowed back in the class.

Henceforth, during the lunch breaks, Nitya started leaving food in her tiffin.

Gradually, she started coming late to school. Often, even her uniform would be soiled and crumpled. While checking her notebook, Ms. Sonika found the hardcover of her notebooks torn. Nitya had no satisfactory answer to it. In fact, she bore all atrocities and punishments without giving any clarification. Standing in punishment outside her class became a routine affair for her. This was a matter of concern for Ms. Sonika and one day, she decided to talk to Nitya. "Meet me after school Nitya!" she commanded.

Ms. Sonika had started noticing a positive change in the girl's attitude as she began to smile and laugh more often but at the same time, Nitya was becoming indisciplined in other aspects. Ms. Sonika was compelled to individually talk to her as she had frequently noticed her collecting the leftover food from her friends and picking biscuit pieces dropped by children after lunch, in her lunch box. There was certainly something strange in her behaviour.

Nitya obediently entered the staffroom and came to Ms. Sonika. The staffroom was echoing with the chattering of teachers. Nitya found them to be noisier than the students. Ms. Sonika made Nitya sit next to her and asked, "What's the matter, child? Do you want me to know something?" Nitya remained silent. Ms. Sonika persuaded her to tell why she was coming late more often than before and of course, the reason behind the foodpicking. Before Nitya could gather the courage to reply, another teacher chirpily interrupted, "Are you going for today's party?" Seeing Ms. Sonika distracted in conversation with the

other teachers, Nitya chose to remain silent and quietly left unnoticed. The behavioural issues with Nitya were brought to the notice of her uncle and aunty who were also unaware about Nitya's reaching late for school. In fact, they informed that Nitya had started returning late from school but they ignored the issue thinking that she perhaps was attending extra classes. Unable to ascertain the reason behind the problem, a concerned Ms. Sonika approached Ms. Handa to find a solution. The teacher apprised the headmistress of the ongoing issues with Nitya and requested her to help. Ms. Handa tried to talk to Nitya but Nitya remained unresponsive. Ms. Handa had always been quite confident that in her strict regime, no student would ever dare to be unpunctual or indisciplined. Nitya had shattered this illusion. The hardest punishments had failed to deter her. So, Ms. Handa decided to probe the issue in another style.

That afternoon, after school was over, Ms. Handa secretly followed Nitya. She noticed that Nitya deviated from the regular route to her house and turned towards a narrow lane. She curiously watched her entering the broken gate of the deserted park that stood secluded from the nearby houses. Its broken boundaries and dry bushes left no doubt that it had remained unattended for quite some time. As Nitya entered the park, four puppies came running towards her and surrounded her. They were wagging their little tails in excitement and trying to cling to her legs. The pups were followed by their weak, injured mother who limped towards Nitya wagging her tail. She snuggled her nose against Nitya's hands and licked her. Nitya cuddled and fondled her and sat on the ground carefree of the dust on her uniform. She caressed the injured leg of the mother dog which was draped with a school sock. Nitya took out her lunch box and laid it open for the dogs to feast upon the leftover food which she had brought for them. The mother dog watched her puppies nibbling and licked Nitya as if thanking her for feeding her pups. The mute animal had gratitude in her eyes for the kind human. Ms. Handa silently watched Nitya and her furry friends love each other. It is when the puppies played and ran in their little kennel that Nitya had built, that Ms. Handa realised that even the hard covers of books could provide shelters to the homeless animals and that true knowledge doesn't necessarily come from books.

Ms. Handa quietly watched with pride that her student excelled in the most important lesson of life, the lesson of kindness.

*****

Charu Gupta